USING
SCIENCE
BE A CRIME SCENE
INVESTIGATOR

By Lorraine Jean Hopping

**Crime Scene Investigator Consultants:
Sharon Plotkin and Christine Kruse–Feldstein**

Series Consultant: Kirk A. Janowiak

ticktock

USING
SCIENCE
BE A CRIME SCENE
INVESTIGATOR

By: Lorraine Jean Hopping
Consultants: Sharon Plotkin and Christine Kruse-Feldstein
Series Consultant: Kirk A. Janowiak
ticktock project editor: Jo Hanks
ticktock designer: Graham Rich
With thanks to: Sara Greasley and Hayley Terry

Copyright © ticktock Entertainment Ltd 2008
First published in Great Britain in 2008 by ticktock Media Ltd.,
Unit 2, Orchard Business Centre, North Farm Road, Tunbridge Wells, Kent, TN2 3XF

ISBN 978 1 84696 620 0 pbk
ISBN 978 1 84696 682 8 hbk
Printed in China

LORRAINE JEAN HOPPING
A former editor of *SuperScience* magazine and The Story of Science book series, Lorraine has authored more than 30 books for children, including *Bone Detective: The Story of Forensic Anthropologist Diane France*, a 2006 NSTA 'Selector's Choice' and 2007 SB&F Young Adult finalist. Other titles for *ticktock* Media include *Investigating a Crime Scene* and *Autopsies and Bone Detectives*.

KIRK A. JANOWIAK
BS Biology & Natural Resources, MS Ecology & Animal Behavior, MS Science Education. Kirk has enjoyed teaching students from preschool through to college age. He has been awarded the National Association of Biology Teachers' Outstanding Biology Teacher Award and was honoured to be a finalist for the Presidential Award for Math and Science Teaching. Kirk currently teaches Biology and Environmental Science and enjoys a wide range of interests from music to the art of roasting coffee.

CSI SHARON PLOTKIN
A crime scene investigator in North Miami, Florida. Sharon has worked thousands of crime scenes including homicides, shootings, armed robberies, and burglaries. Her job involves documenting, collecting, and preserving evidence to be analysed. She and her crime scene unit received the Law Enforcement Officer Award for Best Supporting Services in 2006, the highest award given in law enforcement.

CSI CHRISTINE KRUSE FELDSTEIN
A police officer assigned to the crime scene unit of Miami-Dade, Florida. Christine has handled hundreds of crime scenes ranging from homicides and suicides to armed robberies. She has a passion for photography and new electronics. Though born in Kentucky, Chris considers herself a city girl. She says that you will see her nails scraping on the pavement trying to get her out of the city. She and her crime scene unit received the Law Enforcement Officer Award for Best Supporting Services in 2006, the highest award given in law enforcement.

CONTENTS

This book supports the teaching of science at Key Stage 2 of the National Curriculum. Students will develop their understanding of these areas of scientific inquiry:

- Ideas and evidence in science
- Investigative skills
- Obtaining and presenting evidence
- Considering and evaluating evidence

Students will also learn about:

- Finding and preserving evidence
- Making observations and inferences
- The makeup of blood
- How blood dries and decomposes
- Protecting evidence from moisture, bacteria and mould
- DNA and how it can identify an individual
- Blood types
- Kinetic energy and splash patterns
- Properties of human and animal hairs
- Fingerprint patterns
- Techniques for finding fingerprints
- Comparing shoe and tyre prints
- The composition of soil
- Drawing conclusions based on evidence

HOW TO USE THIS BOOK

Science is important in the lives of people everywhere. We use science at home and at school – in fact, all the time. Everybody needs to know about science to understand how the world works. A crime scene investigator (CSI) needs to understand physics, chemistry, and biology to identify and collect every bit of evidence at a crime scene. Evidence helps detectives solve cases. With this book, you'll use science to examine real types of crime scene evidence in order to solve a made-up case.

This exciting science book is very easy to use – check out what's inside!

INTRODUCTION

Fun to read information about being a crime scene investigator.

FACTFILE

Easy to understand information about how crime scene investigation works.

GETTING THE BLOOD OUT

You're ready to bag and tag the evidence. You start with the most fragile. There's blood outside the door and on the porch. You think the burglar cut themself. 'Hot, sunny day,' you write down. This is good because there's no rain to wash away the blood outside. But it's also bad. The Sun's rays can break down blood. Its heat helps bacteria grow, speeding up the rotting process and destroying your evidence. A trail of blood drops leads from the hallway into the kitchen, where there is a large pool of blood with a knife in the centre. You photograph the scene and move the chair out of your way. Then you grab some cotton swabs and paper evidence bags and go to work.

FACTFILE

Blood that leaves the body begins to change immediately. Blood drops dry from the edges inward. If the centre is still moist, the crime happened recently. The plasma, a pale yellow liquid, separates from the red and white cells. The cells break down and decompose due to bacteria, mould, and other organisms. Heat speeds up this rotting process.

WHAT IS BLOOD?

55%

Plasma: water, sugars, nutrients, acids, salts, minerals, proteins

Less than 1% white blood cells and platelets

WORKSTATION

Real life crime scene investigation experiences, situations and problems for you to read about.

CHALLENGE QUESTIONS

Now that you understand the science, put it into practice.

WORKSTATION

The key to preserving blood evidence is its dryness.

- Do you wonder why bread gets mouldy quickly and yet biscuits last a long time? One big factor is moisture. Mould is a fungus that needs water to grow. Biscuits are drier than bread.

- Likewise, the key to preserving blood evidence is dryness. Investigators use germ-free swabs to pick up wet blood and then let the blood dry completely before bagging it. (Germ-free swabs don't introduce bacteria into the blood.)

- If the blood evidence has already dried, they need to moisten a swab with water in order to pick up a sample. Again, they have to let the swab dry.

- The blood is placed in a paper bag because, unlike a plastic bag, it is not watertight and therefore does not seal in moisture.

CHALLENGE QUESTIONS

1. Of the blood at the crime scene, which should be collected first? Explain.

2. Why is it important to allow collected blood to dry completely before bagging it?

3. Why use a paper bag and not a plastic one?

4. Based on your experience, list three variables, or conditions, that speed up or slow down the drying time of a liquid.

5. How can spilled blood give a clue to the time of a crime?

A

A

11

IF YOU NEED HELP!

TIPS FOR SCIENCE SUCCESS

On page 30 you will find lots of tips to help you with your science work.

ANSWERS

Turn to page 31 to check your answers. (*Try all the activities and questions before you take a look at the answers.*)

GLOSSARY

On page 32 there is a glossary of crime scene investigation words and science words.

YOU'RE ON THE CASE!

'**R**rrrring!' For you, a fresh crime is always one phone call away. You're a crime scene investigator, or CSI for short. You're the person who collects the evidence at a crime scene. What crime will today's call bring? A robbery? A carjacking? Murder? 'Looks like a burglary,' says a police officer over the phone. Break-ins are your most common cases. But then, the officer adds, 'Oh, and there's blood.' Blood? At a burglary? So much for common! Over the phone, you hear unhappy dogs barking. 'Call animal control!' you tell the officer, urgently. 'Keep those dogs away from my evidence!' You grab your tool bag and rush off to the crime scene.

FACTFILE

Both scientists and crime scientists collect and examine evidence. What is evidence? It's a fact that can prove something is true – or not true. It can prove something happened – or didn't happen. In crime science, it can also prove that someone is guilty – or innocent.

Evidence can take the form of a photograph, a document, experiment results, an object, and more. CSIs focus on physical evidence: objects connected to a crime.

Examples of physical evidence: weapons, break-in tools, broken glass, soil, clothes and fibres, blood, hairs, fingerprints, dead bodies.

Physical evidence can be large and obvious, or almost invisible to the naked eye, like this hair.

WORKSTATION

CSIs use four of the five senses to process a crime scene: sight, hearing, smell and touch. Taste isn't used because it is dangerous to taste unknown substances.

- CSIs use tools to extend those senses. A flashlight, magnifying glass, and camera boost eyesight, for example.

- Other tools make collecting or preserving evidence more precise or easier. A ruler that is placed next to an object shows the exact size of the object in a photograph. Sticky tape can pick up tiny hairs and fibres. Bags and containers keep evidence from being spoilt.

MOBILE PHONE   POLICE RADIO   TORCH

MULTI-PURPOSE TOOL   NOTEBOOK
(Includes pliers and a screwdriver)

Q CHALLENGE QUESTIONS

1. How is investigating a crime scene like science?
2. Think: could a sandwich be evidence in a crime case? Explain your answer.
3. Imagine: how might a CSI use their sense of smell at a crime scene? (Remember, the job is about finding and collecting evidence.)

THE INVESTIGATION BEGINS

Pulling up to the crime scene, the first thing you notice isn't what you see. It's what you don't hear: barking. Animal control has secured three English bulldogs offsite; you'll deal with them later. Right now, you focus on searching the crime scene, slowly and carefully, for evidence. You only have one chance to do it right. If clues get ruined or overlooked, there's no way to get them back. A criminal could go free! Where do you start? You observe the entire scene – touching nothing, photographing everything – and make a search plan. Meanwhile, the police interview the victim. 'The only thing missing,' he says, 'is some raw meat!?'

 FACTFILE

Besides gathering evidence, CSIs and scientists share two important skills.

- An observation is knowledge that you gain directly from the scene. In this case, it is noticing the scene's details. Did you see the bowl overturned on the kitchen table (right)? And what is that sticking out of the blood on the floor?

- An inference is indirect knowledge. You gain it from observing details at the scene. No one saw the burglar enter the house. Yet the broken lock (left) tells you someone did – and without using keys!

Communication is an important science skill. When you work on a team, you have to share your knowledge. So CSIs take photos, draw sketches, and make detailed notes.

You sketch the crime scene and all the evidence you think is important. It will help you put together what might have happened. It also helps you remember details that you might otherwise forget after you've left the scene.

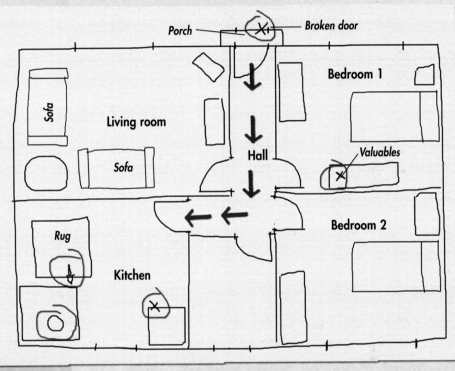

→ The red arrows show the direction you think the burglar walked in.

Q CHALLENGE QUESTIONS

1. What's the difference between an observation and an inference?

2. With a forced entry, what can you infer about the burglar? What does an unforced entry tell you?

3. Observe the crime scene photo on the left. Really study the details! Then, close this book and sketch the room from memory or describe it in writing. When you've included every detail you can remember, look back here to see what you missed.

4. How well could you communicate what you observe at a 'crime scene'? Describe your bedroom in writing. Give the description to a friend who has never been to your home. Can he or she sketch the room based on your notes alone? Try it as many times as you like.

GETTING THE BLOOD OUT

You're ready to bag and tag the evidence. You start with the most fragile. There's blood outside the door and on the porch. You think the burglar cut themself. 'Hot, sunny day,' you write down. This is good because there's no rain to wash away the blood outside. But it's also bad. The Sun's rays can break down blood. Its heat helps bacteria grow, speeding up the rotting process and destroying your evidence. A trail of blood drops leads from the hallway into the kitchen, where there is a large pool of blood with a knife in the centre. You photograph the scene and move the chair out of your way. Then you grab some cotton swabs and paper evidence bags and go to work.

FACTFILE

Blood that leaves the body begins to change immediately. Blood drops dry from the edges inward. If the centre is still moist, the crime happened recently. The plasma, a pale yellow liquid, separates from the red and white cells. The cells break down and decompose due to bacteria, mould, and other organisms. Heat speeds up this rotting process.

WHAT IS BLOOD?

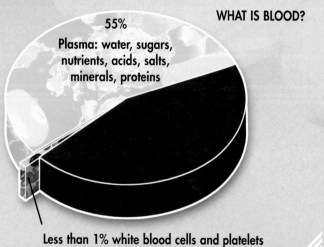

55%
Plasma: water, sugars, nutrients, acids, salts, minerals, proteins

Less than 1% white blood cells and platelets

The key to preserving blood evidence is its dryness.

- Do you wonder why bread gets mouldy quickly and yet biscuits last a long time? One big factor is moisture. Mould is a fungus that needs water to grow. Biscuits are drier than bread.

- Likewise, the key to preserving blood evidence is dryness. Investigators use germ-free swabs to pick up wet blood and then let the blood dry completely before bagging it. (Germ-free swabs don't introduce bacteria into the blood.)

- If the blood evidence has already dried, they need to moisten a swab with water in order to pick up a sample. Again, they have to let the swab dry.

- The blood is placed in a paper bag because, unlike a plastic bag, it is not watertight and therefore does not seal in moisture.

Q CHALLENGE QUESTIONS

1. Of the blood at the crime scene, which should be collected first? Explain.

2. Why is it important to allow collected blood to dry completely before bagging it?

3. Why use a paper bag and not a plastic one?

4. Based on your experience, list three variables, or conditions, that speed up or slow down the drying time of a liquid.

5. How can spilled blood give a clue to the time of a crime?

AT THE CRIME LAB

The samples you collect go to the crime lab for some tests. The first test asks, 'Is it blood?' It turns out that the reddish liquid on the knife and the rug beneath it is animal blood! The burglar probably used the knife to slice the raw meat, and fed it to the bulldogs to calm them. The tests yield other clues, too. All of the blood belonged to a human. None of it belonged to the dogs. The human is a man, with blood type 'O positive'. The last and most important test is for DNA. That takes time. You'll just have to wait for the result.

FACTFILE

- DNA is a super-long strand of chemicals. It's too small to be seen without a powerful microscope.
- Every cell in your body has DNA, except for red blood cells. DNA is in your white blood cells, skin cells and hair roots. It's also in your muscles, fat, bones, and more.
- Your DNA has a different pattern of chemicals than anyone else (unless you have an identical twin). It is one-of-a-kind.
- The lab can tell if DNA found at a crime scene matches a DNA sample from a suspect. A match gives you a direct, physical link between the suspect and the crime scene.

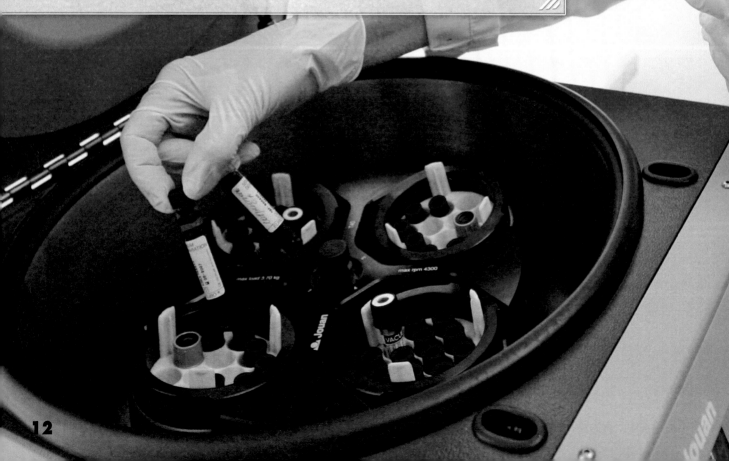

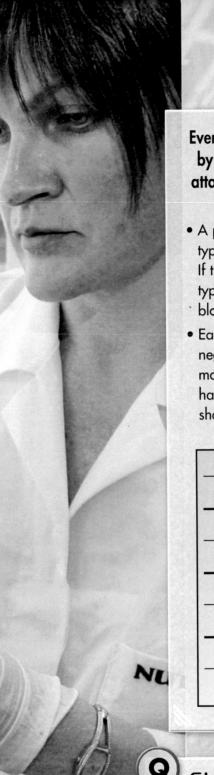

WORKSTATION

Every person has a particular blood type. It is determined by certain chemicals called markers. These markers are attached to a person's red blood cells. Scientists use them to tell what type of blood we have.

- A person's red blood cells can have the markers for blood type A. Or, they can have the markers for blood type B. If they have both sets of markers, that person has blood type AB. If they don't have either set, that person has blood type O.

- Each of these types (A, B, AB, and O) are either positive or negative. 'Positive' means that they have another set of markers called the Rh factor. 'Negative' means they don't have it. Either way, the person's blood is healthy! This chart shows the percentage of people with each blood type:

O	positive	(O+)	38%
O	negative	(O-)	7%
A	positive	(A+)	34%
A	negative	(A-)	6%
B	positive	(B+)	9%
B	negative	(B-)	2%
AB	positive	(AB+)	3%
AB	negative	(AB-)	1%

Q CHALLENGE QUESTIONS

1. If DNA evidence matches the DNA of a suspect, does this put him or her at the scene?

2. The blood at the crime scene is type 'O positive'. What percentage of people have this blood type?

3. The blood belongs to a man. If a male suspect has 'type O positive', does this definitely put him at the scene?

4. Which blood type is a person least likely to have – O, A, B, or AB?

5. What are the only cells in your body that do not contain DNA?

BLOOD IN MOTION

Back at the crime scene, the trail of blood tells a story. It tells you where the burglar walked in the house, and even how fast or slowly. From the front door to the kitchen there are only a few round drops, spaced far apart. The burglar walked straight past some valuables. What was he after? You examine the blood in the kitchen, where blood from his cut dripped. Based on the size of the pool, he stood there for at least a few minutes. He took his time feeding the bulldogs. Why not just throw down some meat and then steal the valuables?

FACTFILE

- Blood flows three to six times more slowly than water.
- As it dries, blood flows even more slowly.

The blood in the kitchen tells you where the burglar stood.

14

Blood doesn't flow or spill or spatter on its own. Forces (such as a blow or gunshot) set it in motion.

Your heartbeat causes your blood to flow. Gravity causes your blood to drop from a wound. The greater the force, the more speed and kinetic energy (the energy something has when it is moving) the blood has.

1

1. High-speed impacts, such as gunshots, have a great deal of kinetic energy. Their energy breaks blood into a mist of very tiny droplets.

2

2. Medium-speed blows, such as a knock on the head, result in small-drop spatter. They have less kinetic energy.

3

3. A swipe is made by a bloody object (like a bleeding hand) touching a clean surface.

4

4. A wipe is made by a clean object touching a pool of blood.

5

5. A drop of blood is shaped like a ball as it falls. When it falls straight down, it creates a circle. Over a long fall, its speed can reach 7.6 metres per second. A fast-falling drop bounces up and out in all directions, creating a 'crown' pattern.

6

6. Blood that lands at an angle forms an oval. The greater the angle, the more stretched-out the oval is. High-speed blood trickles out in a little line after the oval. The drop looks like a tadpole. The arrow points in the direction of the blood's motion.

Q CHALLENGE QUESTIONS

1. What force causes blood to fall straight to the ground?

2. Which blood shown on these pages had the most kinetic energy?

3. How does a lot of kinetic energy change the shape and pattern of blood?

4. What force causes blood to ooze from a wound?

HAIR OF THE DOGS

Your search includes the victim's pets, too. An animal control worker points to the dogs and says, 'Expensive animals, those English bulldogs.' Did the burglar pet one? If so, maybe he picked up dog hairs. Right away, you see that 'pet' isn't the correct word. There's a blood smear on the neck of one of the bulldogs and a clump of hair missing. This looks like an attempted dog-napping! After feeding the dogs, the burglar couldn't grab them. He got scared, dropped the knife, and ran away empty-handed. You collect dog hairs in case they might match hairs found on a suspect. If there ever is a suspect!

FACTFILE

- A head of hair includes several colours, not just one.
- Hair can contain chemicals that a person has taken in, such as drugs, vitamins, or poisons. The closer the chemicals are to the root, the more recently they were absorbed.

WORKSTATION

Crime lab experts examine trace evidence through a microscope. Trace evidence is very small but noticeable. Hair and fibres are trace evidence.

- If it's a hair, is it human or nonhuman? From what part of the body? Was it plucked out or did it fall out? The experts can tell by the angle of the root compared to the shaft.

- There are more than 20 properties of hairs, including:

  - *Length*
  - *Colour (including dyed hair)*
  - *Thickness*
  - *Shape (straight, wavy, curly)*
  - *Texture (rough, smooth)*
  - *Damage*

- It's impossible to match a hair sample to an individual based on these characteristics alone. At best, experts can tell if two hairs are similar to each other – or not.

The hairs on the left are human, and those on the right are dog hairs. They look very different. The dog hair is made up of overlapping scales.

Q CHALLENGE QUESTIONS

1. Take a strand of hair from your hairbrush or comb. Observe your hair. Use a hand lens, if you have one. List three or more properties that you can see.

2. Compare your hair to that of a friend. What properties do they share? What properties are different?

3. Suppose two hairs share 10 properties. Does that mean they came from the same person?

FIND THOSE FINGERPRINTS!

It is impossible to break into a home without touching something. 'Where might fingerprints be lurking?' you wonder. You rarely find visible (patent) prints. They're usually not visible (latent), unless you make them so with chemicals or powders. You can't dust the whole house. So you think, 'What was the burglar likely to touch?' The broken door has no prints; the burglar was probably wearing gloves. Then you remember the missing meat. Sure enough, on the fridge handle, you lift two latent fingerprints. Of course, they could belong to the victim. But if not, bingo!

FACTFILE

- Rub your fingertips with your thumb. How do they feel? Oily? Moist or dry? Sticky or slippery? Skin is coated with sweat, acids, oils, and fats in varying amounts. When you touch something, tiny ridges on your fingers form a pattern made of those substances – a fingerprint pattern.

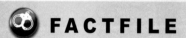

- Sweat is water mixed with salts and other chemicals. The fingerprints of children are more watery than those of adults, and so dry up and lose pattern details faster. Oils stick around for much longer.

- Fingerprints also contain whatever the person recently touched: dirt, pencil marks, food, lotion, or blood (left).

- Everyone's fingerprint patterns are different. So, unlike hairs, fingerprints can link an individual directly to a crime scene.

Making a latent fingerprint visible is called lifting or developing it.

There are a few techniques you can use, depending on the surface.
A porous surface allows moisture to seep in. A nonporous surface is smooth and watertight.

Lifting Technique		Surface
Powder, gently brushed on to the print, clings to oils and fats.		Nonporous (glass, metal, plastic).
A magnetic wand brushes metallic powder over the print. The wand itself doesn't touch the print.		Porous (paper, cardboard, unfinished wood, plaster, drywall).
Ninhydrin is a chemical that turns certain amino acids in the fingerprint pink or purple.		Paper (porous).
Superglue contains a chemical that evaporates. Fumes from the glue stick to fingerprint oils and harden into a white pattern.		Any, but works best on metals and plastics.
Ultraviolet (UV) and other special lights make latent fingerprints glow. Coloured goggles enhance the glow.		Any, but the print has to be developed with powder after the light reveals it.

Q CHALLENGE QUESTIONS

1. Look around the room you are in. List the first five objects you would check for latent fingerprints.

2. Why don't children's fingerprints last as long as adult prints?

3. How do powders make latent fingerprints visible?

4. What technique would you use to reveal a latent print on a paper bank check?

WHOSE PRINTS ARE THEY?

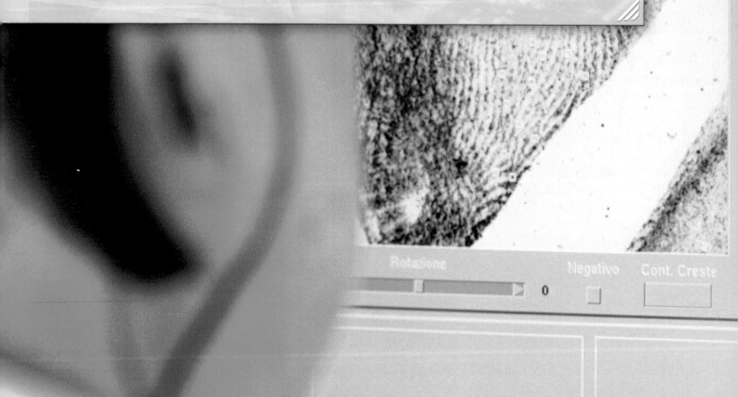

Now that you've scored a couple of fingerprints, what next? How do you find out who made them? You don't. Identifying fingerprints is a tricky job best done by a crime lab. There, a fingerprint specialist examines your prints. He enters the pattern details into a computer data base called AFIS, the Automated Fingerprint Identification System. In the United States, AFIS belongs to the Federal Bureau of Investigation (FBI). Other countries, including the United Kingdom and Australia, have their own AFIS. Will your prints match any of the tens of millions of samples on file? You'll have to wait for the results.

FACTFILE

- Even identical twins have different fingerprints.
- Police use ink, rollers, and white cards (right) to take fingerprints from every suspect who is arrested. They compare these samples to unidentified fingerprints found at crimes scenes. Unless a crime scene print matches a pattern on record, it is useless as evidence.
- Different fingers on the same hand of the same person, can have different patterns or classes of prints. That is why prints are taken of all 10 fingers of an person.

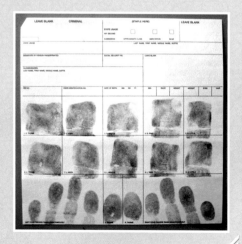

There are three classes of fingerprint patterns: loop, whorl and arch.

A fingerprint can have a mixture of patterns – such as arches across the top and a loop at the core.

Fingerprint:

Symbol that represents the fingerprint:

 Loop   Whorl   Arch

- A **loop** starts and ends on the same side of the fingerprint. It can slant to the right or to the left. About 60 to 65 out of every 100 people have loops.
- A **whorl** has spirals or circles within circles. About 30 out of every 100 people have whorls.
- An **arch** looks like a wave. It starts and ends on opposite sides of the print. Only 5 out of 100 people have arches.

If two prints are in the same class, experts compare one-of-a-kind characteristics such as dots, spurs, and splits called bifurcations. The more points of likeness they find, the stronger the match.

This centre has a dot or island.

At a bifurcation, one ridge splits into two.

A spur is a ridge with a little line sticking out.

Q CHALLENGE QUESTIONS

1. What class does Fingerprint A belong to? Fingerprint B?

2. Observe Fingerprint B. Use a hand lens if you have one. Does it have an island? Can you find a bifurcation?

3. Suppose you spot a patent fingerprint on a glass. What class is the fingerprint most likely to be?

 **A**

 **B**

FOLLOW THE FOOTPRINTS

Fingerprints are great – if you can identify them. But there's another way to link a criminal to a scene. It's one that people often overlook. You don't because your motto is: 'Until people learn how to fly, they have to walk in and out of a crime scene.' That means people leave footprints – or, more often, shoe prints – behind. You search the ground, especially near the entry and exit points. Behind the house, in the soft sand, you find a trail of boot prints. What can these marks reveal about the burglar? You stoop down for a closer look.

FACTFILE

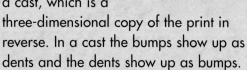

- Some footprints are flat, like the outline of this boot.

- Some footprints are impressions, like the deep print in sand on the right. Here, the CSI is making a cast, which is a three-dimensional copy of the print in reverse. In a cast the bumps show up as dents and the dents show up as bumps.

- An impression is often a little larger than the shoe that made it because the foot slips as it walks.

- Shoe size does not match up well to height. Short people can have big feet!

WORKSTATION

This chart lists the heights and average stride lengths of 11 men and women. Look out for the unusual variations!

Person	Height	Stride
Male	1.89 metres	89cm
Male	1.85 metres	86cm
Male	1.96 metres	86cm
Male	1.82 metres	84cm
Male	1.80 metres	84cm
Female	1.77 metres	81cm
Male	1.74 metres	76cm
Male	1.73 metres	81cm
Female	1.68 metres	74cm
Female	1.60 metres	64cm
Female	1.55 metres	66cm

- Taller people have longer legs and so generally (but not always) take longer strides.
- A stride is the distance between normal walking steps, from the heel of one step to the heel of the next.

Stride length

Q CHALLENGE QUESTIONS

1. If a suspect is 1.65 metres tall, about how long would you predict the stride length to be?

2. The average stride length of the footprints at the crime scene is 81 centimetres. The estimated shoe size is 8 to 10. What does this data tell you about the suspect?

3. Think about how you walk. What might change your stride?

The footprints lead you away from the crime scene to... a new crime scene! Or is it? In the soil by the road behind the house, you find tyre tracks. Did the burglar escape in a car or some other vehicle? Or do these tracks belong to someone else? Were they made before, during, or after the crime? You can't say. The best you can do is photograph and make a cast of the tracks for the crime lab to examine. The lab's experts compare the pattern to hundreds of treads. 'It's a Ford F150 pickup truck,' they soon report. That's helpful. But you wonder: How many people drive Ford F150s? And can the police find the truck that made the tracks?

FACTFILE

When comparing tracks to treads, experts draw three types of conclusions:

1. **Inconclusive, or no match.** The track does not have enough detail for identification.

2. **Class match.** The tread pattern belongs to the tyre of a particular type of vehicle. For example, a Ford F150 truck will have a tyre special to it.

3. **Individual match.** A track has a one-of-a-kind feature. This can be a worn spot or piece of glass in the tread. No two tyres wear exactly the same way. With an individual match, only one truck could have made the track.

Investigators know that the tyre track above was made by the tyre above. Therefore it is a class match.

Tyres have many different combinations of characteristics, which is why it can take a while to identify a track:

CLASS CHARACTERISTICS:

- Tyre circumference (length of the circular tread)
- Width of tread design
- Height of ribs (or depth of grooves)
- Number of ribs
- Width of each rib
- Distance between each rib
- A distinct central rib or not
- Grooves: straight, angled, irregular, or notched

INDIVIDUAL CHARACTERISTICS:

- Worn spots
- Damage (cut, scratch, nail hole)
- Object (pebble, chewing gum) stuck on the tread
- Different brands of tyres on the same vehicle

Tread

Groove (a valley or deep line)　Central rib　Rib (a band that sticks up)

Q CHALLENGE QUESTIONS

1. Do these tyres have similar grooves?
2. What is different about the ribs? List two things.
3. Is it more likely to make an individual match with an old tyre or a new one? Explain why.

A　B

4. You can compare the tread patterns of shoes to make a class or individual match. Observe your treads. How do your soles compare to those of your friends? Can you find a class match (the same brand of shoe)?
5. Name three to five properties that would make your tread an individual match to your shoe print.

BITS AND PIECES

Isn't it great how one piece of evidence leads to another? Footprints led you to tyre tracks. Now you observe unusual soil in the tyre tracks. This is good – unusual makes it easier to narrow down suspects. The soil is colourful beach sand with dark granules, bits of white shell and seeds – there isn't a beach nearby! You scoop up a sample to send to the crime lab. Whew! You're done. That's the last clue to collect at the scene. Even so, you always worry, 'Is there enough evidence?' Time (and the next two pages) will tell.

FACTFILE

Soil comes in nearly 1,100 colours! The colour depends on the minerals and other contents. For example, iron oxide (rust) adds a reddish tint. Sea salt is white. Crushed lava rock from a volcano can form very black sand.

This is a picture of beach sand.

This is a 15x magnified picture of sand.

WORKSTATION

Soil is made up of many different bits.

In a beaker of water, the heaviest bits sink to the bottom and the lightest pieces settle on top. Weight is the property that causes this separation, and gravity is part of the effect. This soil is classified as 'sandy loam' due to the relative amounts of sand, silt, and clay.

This layer is water.

This layer is clay (topped with a few other bits).

The middle layer is silt.

About two-thirds of the solid material in the sample is sand.

Bits of soil are classified by size, as shown here:

 Boulders: Greater than 256mm

 Cobbles: 64-256mm

 Pebbles: 4-64mm

 Granules: 2-4mm

 Very coarse sand: 1-2mm

 **Coarse sand:** 0.5-1mm

 Medium sand: 0.25-0.5mm

 Fine sand: 0.1-0.25mm

 Very fine sand: 0.05-0.1mm

 Silt: 0.002-0.05mm

 Clay: Less than 0.002mm

Q CHALLENGE QUESTIONS

1. Suppose most of the bits measure about 3mm. What type of soil is it, according to the chart above?

2. The soil in the beaker separates into layers according to what property?

3. Which layer in the beaker has the smallest bits?

4. What fraction of the solid material in the beaker is silt and clay?

5. Why does unusual soil narrow down the possible suspects?

WEIGH THE EVIDENCE

You barely return to your office when . . . Yrrrring! 'I think we've got your dog-napper,' says an officer over the phone. That was fast! 'Get this,' she adds. 'He drives a Ford F150 pickup. And he has a cut on his wrist. There's blood on the truck!' Is he guilty? No one can tell from those facts alone. You and a jury will have to look at all the evidence. Speaking of which, you grab your tool bag and head out to check the suspect and his truck for new clues. Who knows? He could be innocent.

WORKSTATION

This is a list of the evidence you have collected during your investigation:

Evidence collected about suspect	Evidence collected at the crime scene	
The suspect is 1.78 metres tall.	The stride lengths of the footprints predict someone a few centimetres smaller.	
His blood type is O positive.	The blood type found at the scene is O positive.	
His fingerprints don't match those found in the house.	One fingerprint at the crime scene matches the victim. The other is unknown.	
The suspect's truck contains a crowbar and rubber gloves.	The front door was forced open. Latent fingerprints were found.	
The suspect drives a Ford F150.	The truck's tyres are a class match to the tracks at the scene but not an individual match.	
Soil is found on the tyres of the suspect's F150.	The soil on the tyres is not consistent with the soil at the crime scene.	
The suspect is wearing boots.	The suspect's boots are a class and size match to the footprints. The boots are a common brand.	
Dog hairs are found on the suspect.	The properties of the hairs are consistent with several breeds, including English bulldogs.	
Blood is found in the Ford F150.	The blood on the Ford F150 pickup truck and at the scene match DNA samples from the suspect.	

Q CHALLENGE QUESTIONS

Based on the evidence, do you think he is guilty or innocent?

- Read through all the evidence carefully before you decide.
- List evidence that points to guilt in one column and innocence in another column. Leave out any evidence that isn't helpful either way.
- Weigh the evidence: which clue is the most important?

29

TIPS FOR SCIENCE SUCCESS

Pages 6-7

You're on the Case

Just as a CSI and a scientist would, stay focused on the evidence throughout this book. You'll use all of it to solve this (made-up) burglary case.

Pages 8-9

The Investigation Begins

For many of the questions in this book, the answers are open-ended. Unlike maths problems, there's often no single, correct answer in science. You and a friend can make two different observations that are both true. The key is to always check what you think is true against what you see. Stick to the evidence. In this case, the evidence is what you can see in the picture. When describing objects in your room, think about these properties: location, size, shape, colour, pattern, material, and texture (smooth or rough, for example).

Pages 10-11

Getting the Blood Out

CSI Sharon Plotkin says: 'If you want to know why wet items should be packaged in paper, think of a wet bathing suit placed in a plastic bag at the beach. If you forget to take it out when you get home, what happens? When you find it a couple of days later, the suit smells bad and has black spots all over it – these are mould or mildew.'

Pages 14-15

Blood in Motion

What causes your blood to flow throughout your body? Here's a hint: dead people don't bleed. Their blood stops circulating the moment they die.

Pages 16-17

Hair of the Dogs

A property is a characteristic that describes an object, such as its colour. The more detailed the description, the more exact the comparison is. There are thousands of colours beyond red, yellow, and blue! If two hairs share certain properties, they are consistent with each other (to use a CSI phrase). That means they are similar, but it doesn't mean they came from the same source.

Pages 18-19

Find Those Fingerprints!

Oils, fats, and waxes belong to a group of substances called lipids. Lipids don't dissolve in water. (Have you heard the expression, 'Oil and water don't mix?') The difference is the state of matter: oils are liquids, fats are soft semisolids, and waxes are hard solids.

Pages 20-21

Whose Prints Are They?

Classes are groups of items that share a characteristic, such as fingerprint ridges shaped like an arch. A subclass is a group within a group, such as arches with a little peak in the middle – or tented arches. Most fingerprint experts use three classes and five subclasses.

Pages 22-23

Follow the Footprints

Is there a relationship between height and stride length? To answer questions like that, scientists compare two sets of data in a chart or graph and look for a pattern. Not every number has to fit the pattern exactly. The more data collected, the better the comparison is.
To help answer question three, walk shoulder-to-shoulder with a friend who's taller or smaller than you. Take at least 10 steps together, taking care to walk as naturally as possible.

Pages 24-25

Getaway Tracks

You can do more than observe the tyres. Count the ribs (the bands that stick up) and the grooves (the valleys or deep lines).

Pages 28-29

Bits and Pieces

Evidence is rarely clear-cut. The tyre tracks are a class match, but millions of people drive Ford F150 trucks. Ditto for the boots: they're common. Does the lack of a fingerprint match mean the suspect is innocent? What if he wore gloves? Or cleaned his prints?

Pages 6-7

1. They're both about collecting and examining evidence.
2. Yes, any object can be evidence if it's used as proof.
3. Answers will vary. Smell can help CSIs find or identify unknown substances such as food, petrol, perfume, and so on.

Pages 8-9

1. An observation is direct; an inference is indirect.
2. A burglar without a key is likely to be a stranger. An unforced entry points to friends or family with keys.
3 and 4. The more you practise these exercises, the better you will get. Try them over again and keep track of your score.

Pages 10-11

1. The blood outside the porch and door is the most fragile because it's exposed to the Sun. Also, once the CSI enters the house, it's out of eyesight and could be accidentally destroyed.
2. To avoid trapping moisture inside, which would allow mould or bacteria to grow.
3. Plastic is watertight – it seals in moisture.
4. In this case you're worried about: temperature (the Sun), exposure to air and moisture.
5. The amount of drying, the separation of plasma from cells, and decomposition (rotting) are clues to the time of the crime.

Pages 12-13

1. Yes. It could only belong to one person because everyone's DNA is different.
2. 38%.
3. The suspect could have been at the scene, but as 38% of the population is O+, it could have been any one of them!
4. AB.
5. Red blood cells.

Pages 14-15

1. Gravity.
2. Picture 1: the gunshot spatter.
3. The force breaks blood drops into a fine mist.
4. A beating heart pumps blood through your body and out of open wounds.

Pages 16-17

1 and 2. Answers will vary. Use the clipboard list as a guide.
3. No. It just means the hairs are similar.

Pages 18-19

1. Answers will vary. Examples: entrances and exits, handles, knobs, on-off switches, computer keyboards, and other objects that are often picked, or held, or opened and closed.
2. They have a higher water content. The water evaporates quickly.
3. By sticking to oils and fats.

4. Magnetic wand or ninhydrin. (Paper is porous.)

Pages 20-21

1. Fingerprint A is a whorl. Fingerprint B is a loop.

2.

One of many bifurcations.

Island

3. A loop.

Pages 22-23

1. About 71 centimetres, give or take a few centimetres. There isn't an exact answer to this question.
2. Careful! You can't tell male versus female by this data. The stride length suggests a height of about 1.73 metres to 1.75 metres. Shoe size is not a clue to height.
3. Walking faster or slower than normal, taking extra small or larger steps, walking uphill, or over bumpy ground.

Pages 24-25

1. No, the grooves on tyre B have a small square set in to them.
2. They are a different width, distance apart and height. They also have a different pattern.
3. An old tyre – because wear and tear will create individual marks. (The samples are new tyres.)
4. Answers will vary.
5. Any odd mark that belongs only to the individual shoe.

Pages 26-27

1. Granules.
2. Weight.
3. Clay.
4. One-third is silt and clay.
5. More suspects would have common soil on them than unusual or rare soil.

Pages 28-29

He's guilty! The DNA in the blood is the best proof because it's an individual match. The tyre, boot, and dog hairs are class matches that support the verdict, but they are less exact. The fingerprints, the soil, and the stride lengths don't prove innocence or guilt.

AMINO ACIDS Chemicals in the body that make up proteins.

BACTERIA A variety of microscopic organisms made of one cell. Many bacteria decompose dead plant and animal matter.

BURGLARY A break-in when no one is at home. If someone is in the home, the crime is a home invasion. A threat of harm, such as a gun or knife, makes it a robbery.

CLASS A group with shared characteristics. Scientists classify plants, animals, and objects into classes.

CONSISTENT WITH Similar to, but not an exact or individual match. Two hairs with similar properties are consistent with each other, but they don't necessarily come from the same source.

DATA Information, such as measurements or experiment results, collected in a scientific investigation.

DECOMPOSITION Rotting due to the presence of mould, bacteria, other organisms, weather and temperature.

DIAMETER The distance across the centre of a circle. The diameter of a hair is equal to its greatest width.

DNA: A molecule present in many living cells which gives the instructions for making a plant, animal, or other organism.

Each human's DNA is unique, unless they are an identical twin.

EVAPORATE Turn from liquid state into a gas state.

FIBRE A thread from clothing material, a carpet, furniture, and so on.

KINETIC ENERGY The energy of motion. A fast-moving object has more kinetic energy than a slow-moving object of the same mass.

LATENT Invisible to the eye. The term applies to any evidence, not just fingerprints.

PATENT Visible to the eye.

PRESERVE Save or protect from damage or harm, especially from bacteria and other decomposers.

POROUS A material that has really small spaces that air or water can pass through.

PROPERTY A trait or characteristic of an object.

TRACE EVIDENCE Small evidence such as hairs, fibres, pieces of glass, paint chips, and so on.

VARIABLE A factor or condition that changes a result. For example, wind and temperature are two variables that affect how fast a liquid dries up.

PICTURE CREDITS

(l=left, r=right, t=top, c=centre, b=bottom, f=far)

Alamy 2tc, 8-9 (main), 10-11 (main), 11tr, 11br, 18-19 (main), 19b, 22-23 (main), 24-25 (foreground), 24-25 (background), 26-27 (main), 28-29 (main). Brand X ofc (main). Getty 6-7 (main). Lorraine Jean Hopping 8bl. Michael Karlsson/arrestingimages.com 6br. National Science Foundation: Greg Greico, Penn State 19cb. Ron Smith 24bl, 24br. Science Photo Library 1 (main), 12-13 (main), 14-15 (main), 17cl, 17cr, 19ct, 19t, 20-21 (main), 26bl, 27tr, 29cb, 29fb. Sharon Plotkin 7c, 15bl. 15cr, 15br, 19c, 19bc, 22c, 30br. Shutterstock obc tl, obc br, 11cr, 12cr, 14-15 (main), 14cl, 15tl, 15tr, 16-17 (main), 20br, 21c, 21br, 25tr, 25bl, 25br, 26cl, 29ft, 29b, 29t, 30-31 (main), 31tr, 32 (main). Teddy Harley 21bl. Ticktock Media Archive 9cr, 10bl, 15cl, 15tr, 21tl, 21tc, 21tr, 23c, 27c (all), 29ct.

Every effort has been made to trace the copyright holders, and we apologise in advance for any unintentional omissions.

We would be pleased to insert the appropriate acknowledgments in any subsequent edition of this publication.